J 978.02 TRA
3525100128A569
12y
Sonneborn, Liz
The Mormon Trail

W9-AFN-835

The Mormon Trail

The Mormon Trail

Liz Sonneborn

Franklin Watts
A Division of Scholastic Inc.
New York • Toronto • London • Auckland • Sydney
Mexico City • New Delhi • Hong Kong
Danbury, Connecticut

Note to readers: Definitions for words in **bold** can be found in the Glossary at the back of this book.

Photographs © 2005: AP/Wide World Photos: 52 (Barry Beard/The Vicksburg Post), 31 (Utah Historical Society); Brown Brothers: 17, 18; Corbis Images: 30 (James L. Amos), 5 bottom, 6, 20, 24, 36, 38, 40, 48, 50 (Bettmann), 2 (Gordon Whitten), 32, 43, 46; Craig James Ostler, Department of Church History and Doctrine, Brigham Young University: 41; LDS Church Archives: 47 (Charles Roscoe Savage), 37; Library of Congress: 14 (Chas B. Hall), 9; Mary Evans Picture Library: 26; National Park Service: 51; North Wind Picture Archives: 5 top, 15 (Nancy Carter), 28, 33, 34, 42; Robertstock.com/Retrofile.com: 12; Stock Montage, Inc.: cover, back cover ghost, 49; The Image Works/Topham: 10; Used by permission, Utah State Historical Society, all rights reserved: 19 (George M. Ottinger), 22, 39, 44.

The photograph on the cover shows a caravan of Mormons.
The photograph opposite the title page shows a purple-hued mesa along the Mormon Trail in Utah.

Library of Congress Cataloging-in-Publication Data

Sonneborn, Liz.
    The Mormon Trail / Liz Sonneborn.
        p. cm. — (Watts library)
    Includes bibliographical references and index.
    ISBN 0-531-12317-0
    1. Mormon pioneers—West (U.S.)—History—Juvenile literature. 2. Frontier and pioneer life—West (U.S.)—Juvenile literature. 3. Mormon Church—United States—History—19th century—Juvenile literature. 4. Mormon Pioneer National Historic Trail—History—Juvenile literature. 5. West (U.S.)—History—19th century—Juvenile literature. I. Title. II. Series.
    F593.S698 2005
    978—dc22   2005001466

© 2005 by Liz Sonneborn.
All rights reserved. Published simultaneously in Canada.
Printed in the United States of America.
1 2 3 4 5 6 7 8 9 10 R 14 13 12 11 10 09 08 07 06 05

Contents

An American family heading west stops for a rest.

Chapter One

The Saints

In the nineteenth century, about a half million Americans headed to lands in what is now the western United States. All believed that they would find a better life in the West. Many wanted to settle the free and fertile farmland there. Others were lured by the easy riches they hoped to discover in gold and silver mines.

Some, however, were not drawn to the West by land, gold, or silver. Instead, they hoped to find the freedom to worship as they wished. Among them were the Mormons. Between 1846 and 1869, more than seventy thousand Mormons made the overland journey from Illinois to what is now Utah. The path they followed became known as the Mormon Trail.

A New Religion

The story of the Mormons began in Manchester, New York, in 1820. The area around Manchester was known as the Burnt-Out District. Many people who lived there were poor farmers. Hungry and desperate, they lost faith in older religions. They began looking for hope in new religious beliefs.

Among them was a fourteen-year-old boy named Joseph Smith. One day, he began to pray, asking God to guide him. Years later, Smith described that moment: "I . . . began to offer up the desires of my heart to God. . . . I saw a pillar of light exactly over my head, above the brightness of the sun, which descended gradually until it fell upon me." In Smith's vision, God told him to reject all the religions he had heard about. In time, God explained, Smith himself would discover "the one true" Christian faith.

Smith had many more visions. During one, an angel led him to several golden plates covered with ancient writing. Although Smith had little education, he spent years translating them. His translations were published in The Book of Mormon in 1830. The same year, he and five other men founded the Church of Christ. (It was later renamed the Church of Jesus Christ of Latter-day Saints.) Members of the church called themselves Saints. Those outside the church more often referred to them as Mormons.

Mormons and Gentiles

Many non-Mormons became suspicious of Smith and his religion. They were particularly upset by his claims that he had received **revelations** from God. These non-Mormons—called Gentiles by Smith—began threatening his followers. To escape **persecution,** the Mormons left New York and headed west, first to Ohio, then to Missouri. Smith's church continued to grow, but wherever the Mormons went, they felt unwelcome. Slave owners in Missouri were especially hostile because Mormons opposed slavery. Fighting soon broke out between the Missouri Mormons and their Gentile neighbors.

Missouri's governor, Lilburn Boggs, sided with the non-Mormons. On October 27, 1838, he issued an **Extermination** Order. It said that if the Mormons did not leave Missouri, they would be killed by the state **militia.** Three days later, the militiamen killed seventeen Mormons. Smith was placed in jail. While he was imprisoned, a young church leader named Brigham Young led

Joseph Smith receives the revelations that lead him to establish the Church of Christ.

the Missouri Mormons across the Mississippi River into Illinois. Smith escaped from jail and joined them the following spring.

Nauvoo

The Mormons established a new settlement near the town of Commerce, Illinois. The area's swamplands seemed an unlikely site for the center of the Mormon Church. But Nauvoo, the city Smith founded there, prospered. Within five years, its population exploded from one thousand to more than ten thousand.

The Mormons worked hard to make Nauvoo successful. A symbol of their dedication was the city's temple. In 1841, construction began on this great structure, high on a hill overlooking Nauvoo. Church leaders asked all Mormons to do whatever they could to help fund the project. A Mormon woman named Elizabeth Kirby wrote in 1843 of the sacrifices she made: "I could not think of anything that would grieve me to part with in my possession, except Francis Kirby's [her deceased husband's] watch. So, I gave it to help build the Nauvoo Temple and everything else that I could possibly spare."

The Mormon Temple at Nauvoo

10

As Nauvoo grew, so did Smith's power. Smith ruled over thousands of people and assembled a large military force. As before, non-Mormons living nearby became wary of Smith and his followers. Fueling their feelings was the church leaders' practice of being married to more than one woman at the same time. Mormons called this practice **plural marriage.** (The Mormon Church officially ended the practice of plural marriage in 1890.)

A few Mormons were also fearful of Smith. In the spring of 1844, they published their anti-Smith views in a newspaper, the *Nauvoo Expositor*. Under Smith's orders, the *Expositor*'s printing press was destroyed. Because of the incident, Illinois's governor imprisoned Joseph Smith. On June 27, a mob of about two hundred non-Mormons charged the jail and shot the Mormon leader to death. Smith's brother Hyrum, who had been imprisoned with him, was also killed.

Smith's followers were devastated. As one Mormon wrote, "A cloud of gloom was spread over the People and Sorrow depicted in every face." Smith's murder not only left them without a leader. It also left them believing that no Mormon was safe in Illinois. They decided to leave Nauvoo.

Smith for President

Early in 1844, Joseph Smith announced that he would run for president of the United States. He intended to choose fellow Mormon Sidney Rigdon as his running mate. Smith's campaign ended with his murder on June 27, 1844.

Brigham Young, the Mormon leader after Joseph Smith's death

Chapter Two

To Zion

After the death of Joseph Smith, the Mormons turned to Brigham Young for leadership. At age forty-three, Young was the president of the Quorum of Twelve, which is also known as the Council of Twelve Apostles. This organization had been established by Smith to help govern the Mormon Church.

Under Young, the Mormons worked hard to complete the great temple at Nauvoo. But they knew they could not stay in the city for long. All the while, they scrambled to prepare for their departure. The Mormons sold their land. They built wagons. They bought tools,

The Mormons leave Nauvoo, Illinois.

weapons, and clothing. Still, the Mormons feared they would be attacked before they were ready to leave. Young tried to calm the growing tensions between the Mormons and non-Mormons. He promised the non-Mormons his people would be out of Illinois by the spring of 1846.

Leaving Nauvoo

For the Mormons' enemies, however, spring was not soon enough. Their threats grew louder. In early February 1846, Young believed the Mormons had to leave Illinois, whether they were ready or not. During a cold winter night, the first group of Mormons fled Nauvoo and crossed the Mississippi River into Iowa **Territory.**

Outfitting a Wagon

On October 29, 1845, a Nauvoo newspaper published a list of supplies every family needed before heading west. The list included:

- one strong wagon
- two or three pairs of oxen
- 1,000 pounds (454 kilograms) of flour
- one musket or rifle for each male over the age of twelve
- 25 pounds (11 kg) of salt
- 5 pounds (2 kg) of dried peaches
- 20 pounds (9 kg) of soap
- 25 to 100 pounds (11 to 45 kg) of tools
- a sturdy tent and furniture

Restored covered wagons can be seen at Scotts Bluff National Monument located on the Oregon Trail in Nebraska.

This advance team included several thousand Mormons. They called themselves the Camp of Israel. These Mormons likened themselves to the biblical Israelites, who wandered the desert looking for a promised land they called **Zion.**

The Mormons hoped to find their Zion in the West. Before leaving Nauvoo, Young studied maps and guidebooks that described routes to western lands. The most popular route was the Oregon Trail. Since 1841, thousands of Americans in **wagon trains** had followed this trail to the rich farmland of Oregon Territory. Young considered settling his people in present-day Oregon or California. As Mormons began their western trek, however, their leaders still were not sure where they were headed.

Going West

The uncertainty was hard on the Camp of Israel. But even more difficult were their living conditions. In eastern Iowa Territory, they set up Sugar Camp. At this settlement, they waited until the weather was warm enough to travel. With 6 inches (15 centimeters) of snow on the ground, they struggled to stay warm in **flimsy** tents. To keep up their spirits, camp members danced to music played by a brass band.

In early March, the Camp of Israel began its march westward across Iowa Territory. The trip was exhausting. Heavy rains made travel slow and kept the camp members wet and cold. The horses and oxen suffered as well. Because there was little grass on the route, the starving animals had nothing to eat but tree limbs and bark.

Despite their misery, the camp members faithfully obeyed their leaders. Young demanded strict discipline. He told his followers, "It will not do to start off helter-skelter without order and decorum [proper behavior]—if we should, but few would reach the place of destination."

Young also demanded that the camp members work hard to improve the trail. Along the way, they built cabins, constructed bridges, dug wells, and plowed and planted fields. These were all meant to be used by the Mormons left in

Crossing Iowa Territory

The Camp of Israel took four months to travel from Nauvoo, Illinois, to the Missouri River.

Mormons working together to build a bridge

Illinois who would travel west later. Camp of Israel members also established three settlements—Locust Creek, Garden Grove, and Mount Pisgah—as way stations where later travelers could rest.

The Poor Saints

On June 14, 1846, the Camp of Israel arrived at the Missouri River on the western edge of Iowa Territory. Crossing the Missouri, they established a settlement in present-day Nebraska. It became known as Winter Quarters.

Young had wanted to complete the journey west before the cold weather set in. But that no longer seemed possible. By then, the trail across Iowa was flooded with thousands of Mormons who had fled Nauvoo soon after the Camp of Israel left. Winter Quarters would give them all a place to stay when the weather became too cold and snowy to travel.

Thousands of Wagons

The Mormons used more than 3,500 wagons to make their journey west.

Mormon encampment on the Mississippi River

By the end of August, Nauvoo was nearly deserted. There were only about eight hundred Mormons left in the city. They were either too sick to travel or too poor to buy a wagon and supplies. Church members called them the Poor Saints. Now outnumbered by non-Mormons in their own city, the Poor Saints were attacked by an angry mob. They were forced out of Nauvoo into makeshift camps on the west bank of the Mississippi River. One eyewitness described the scene: "Dreadful indeed, was the suffering of these forsaken beings. . . . They were there because they had no homes, nor hospitals, nor poor house, no friends to offer them any." From there, the Poor Saints began their trek across Iowa, hurrying to reach Winter Quarters before the weather turned.

For those who survived, Winter Quarters offered few comforts. The winter of 1846–47 was unusually harsh. The Mormons at Winter Quarters and other nearby camps had only thin cotton tents to protect them from the bitter wind. As their supplies dwindled, many went hungry or became ill with deadly diseases. At the camps, more than six hundred Mormons died, still many miles from Zion.

The Mormon
Battalion

The Mormon Battalion

While the Mormons were traveling across present-day Iowa, the United States declared war on Mexico. Needing soldiers, U.S. officials asked Brigham Young for help. In 1846, Young agreed to provide five hundred men for the Mormon Battalion. In exchange, the U.S. government allowed Young to set up winter camps on Indian land along both banks of the Missouri. Young also welcomed the soldiers' pay, which the church could use to bring more Mormons west.

The Mormons nearly always obeyed their leaders. But few men were eager to volunteer for the Mormon Battalion. They bitterly remembered that the U.S. government had done nothing to stop mobs from killing Mormons and destroying their homes. As one Mormon man said, "[T]o call on us to help fight [the United States'] battles to me it was an insult." Nevertheless, Young was able to recruit a full battalion. Its members helped forge new trails throughout the West during and after the war.

The Pioneer Band heads west.

Chapter Three

The Pioneer Band

By April, spring had arrived at Winter Quarters. Brigham Young announced it was time for the Mormons to continue their journey west. To lead the way, he assembled the Pioneer Band. This group of 147 would blaze a trail for the rest of the Mormons to follow.

The Pioneer Band marched out of the Mormons' winter camp on April 16, 1847. Young decided the route they would take. The popular Oregon Trail followed the south bank of the Platte

River. But Young commanded his group to head along the river's north bank instead. This route had long been used by Indians and non-Indian traders. Few wagon trains chose it, however, because it had little grazing land for the animals. Even so, the less-traveled path was attractive to the Mormons. They were happy to avoid non-Mormons because, in the past, contact with them had so often led to violence.

Blazing the Trail

Young set out strict rules for the Pioneer Band. At about five o'clock in the morning, a bugle sounded. This signaled it was

William Clayton

time to wake up, get dressed, eat breakfast, and say their morning prayers. By seven, the wagons had to be packed and ready to roll. The wagon trains traveled for twelve hours or more before stopping for the night. Bedtime was at nine, following evening prayers. The travelers wanted to be well-rested for the next day.

Young assigned special jobs to members of the Pioneer Band. For example, William Clayton was asked to keep a written record of the journey.

In it, he wrote down how many miles they covered each day. To measure distance, Clayton tied a piece of red cloth to a wagon wheel and counted how many times it made a complete circle. After the cloth had gone around 360 times, the wagon had traveled a mile. For days, Clayton watched the wheel and counted. (Friends finally developed a simple machine to count wheel turns so Clayton would be relieved of this boring job.) Clayton later published his records and measurements into a guidebook. It helped thousands of Mormons and non-Mormons follow the Pioneer Band's trail.

Not all of the members were as devoted to duty as Clayton. As the days wore on, they began looking for ways to amuse themselves. Many men began hunting the buffalo that roamed the plains. A few hunted even when they did not need meat, even though Mormonism forbade killing animals for sport. Some also passed the time in camp playing cards, wrestling, and joking with one another. Young became furious. He thought their behavior was inappropriate, considering their sacred mission.

On May 29, 1847, Young gathered the Pioneer Band together. He said he would not go any farther unless they changed their ways. "If we don't repent and quit our wickedness," Young threatened, "we will have more hindrances than we have had and worse storms to encounter." The men promised to behave. As one noted, after Young's speech, "no loud laughter was heard, no swearing, no profane language, no hard speeches to man or beast."

Come, Come Ye Saints

To keep their spirits high, the Pioneer Band sang "Come, Come Ye Saints." One verse celebrated the new home they hoped to find:

"We'll find the place which God for us prepared, Far away in the West; Where none shall come to hurt or make afraid; There the Saints will be blessed.

We'll make the air with music ring— Shout praises to our God and king; Above the rest these words we'll tell—All is well! All is well!"

Famous mountain man Jim Bridger

Exploring the West

Jim Bridger was probably the first non-Indian to see Great Salt Lake, in present-day northern Utah.

Meeting Jim Bridger

Fully focused on finding Zion, the Pioneer Band continued on its way. By early June, the group reached Fort Laramie, an old trading post. There, they decided to cross over to the south side of the Platte River. Some **ferried** wagons of other travelers across the river for a fee. Young saw a way to help finance the trip west for other Mormons. He asked several members to stay behind and run a ferrying business.

The rest of the group soon reached the Rocky Mountains. They led their wagons through South Pass, the place where the mountain range was easiest to cross. As they traveled on, they ran into Jim Bridger. He was a famous mountain man—a trader who had explored trails throughout the West.

Young and other Mormon leaders spent hours talking with Bridger. They wanted his advice on where they should go and how best to get there. During their conversation, Bridger said they should definitely stay away from Great Salt Lake. This enormous lake was a few hundred miles away in what is now northern Utah. Bridger said it was too cold to farm in the area. He was so sure, he offered $1,000 to anyone who could grow an ear of corn there.

Entering the Valley

Young, however, had made up his mind. Despite Bridger's report, he decided to head toward the valley of Great Salt Lake. On July 4, the Pioneer Band arrived at Fort Bridger, a post Jim Bridger had built. From there, the Oregon Trail veered northwest. Young led his people on a path that headed southwest. The trail they followed was described in *The Emigrant's Guide to Oregon and California* by Lanford B. Hastings. Trusting Hastings's guidebook was risky. The previous winter, the Donner Party had taken a route that Hastings recommended. About half of the eighty-nine members of the party died after being trapped for months in the snowy mountains.

Three weeks later, the Pioneer Band entered the valley. Though located in the desert, it was well watered by brooks and small rivers full of trout. It was also full of tall grass, perfect for grazing animals. One Mormon claimed that "if [the valley] could receive timely rains, it would be one of the most beautiful, fertile regions on the face of the earth."

On July 24, 1847, the travelers caught their first full view of Great Salt Lake. Young knew immediately their journey was over. As he later explained, "The Spirit of Light rested upon me, and hovered over the valley, and I felt that there the saints would find protection and safety."

Finding Zion

According to some histories of the Mormon faith, when Brigham Young saw Salt Lake Valley, he declared, "This is the place."

The Mormon settlement at Salt Lake City, Utah, in 1847

Chapter Four

Mormons and Miners

Once the Mormons reached their new home, they worked to establish a city. Houses had to be built, and fields had to be cleared and planted.

Within weeks of their arrival, Young and several other leaders left Salt Lake. Traveling east along the Mormon Trail, they set off for Winter Quarters. There, they organized three wagon trains that carried about 2,400 Mormons west. Over the next two years, thousands more would make the trek.

Salt Lake City grew quickly in the late 1840s.

Mormon Settlements

In addition to Salt Lake City, the Mormons eventually founded more than 350 settlements in the American West.

The Mormons expected to live undisturbed in Salt Lake Valley. The region was largely unsettled. It was then part of Mexico, but few people lived there. Within months of the Mormons' arrival, however, Mexico lost a war with the United States. In the peace treaty, the United States purchased much of Mexico's territory, including the Mormons' new homeland. The Mormons knew this meant that more Americans would be coming to their lands. But no one could have predicted just how many people would soon be traveling on the western trails.

The Gold Rush

In January 1848, gold was found in what is now northern California. As news of the discovery spread, hundreds of thousands of Americans decided to head west. All were sure they could find enough gold in California to make them rich. Because most set out in 1849, the would-be gold miners were nicknamed forty-niners.

Most of the forty-niners traveled in wagon trains along the Oregon and California trails. They rushed along these routes, eager to get to California before the gold ran out. Many started off without gathering enough food and supplies for the trip.

For hundreds of miles, the Oregon Trail followed the south bank of the Platte River. Some forty-niners decided to cross the Platte to travel on the less-crowded Mormon Trail. They shared the route with the Mormons flooding out of Winter Quarters.

"The Hardships of This Journey"

While traveling to California during the **gold rush,** forty-niner Edward Jackson kept a diary that included this description of traveling on the Mormon Trail:

"The hardships of this journey . . . cannot be written. You should hear it from the mouth and then you could not realize the fatigues & deprivations of a journey which would take the life of a common man. In the morning, cold bracing wind, with pure crystal water—in the afternoon sultry air, if any and water impregnated with alkali, or some mineral substance, to quench the thirst. These are the extremes we often suffer."

The Mormons were not always pleased to be traveling alongside the miners. The heavy traffic along the trail left little grass for their animals to eat. Many travelers from the East also carried diseases. Particularly deadly was **cholera.** As cholera spread through the wagon trains, graves became a common site along the trail. One traveler recalled that his father began counting the graves when their family left Winter Quarters. The man gave up counting after he reached one thousand.

This pile of stones marks a pioneer grave along the trail.

To Salt Lake City

After traveling through South Pass, most forty-niners took the Sublette Cutoff. This trail fed directly into the California Trail, which led to the California gold mines. Some miners, however, chose to bypass the Sublette Cutoff. They instead headed south on the Mormon Trail to Salt Lake City.

In the Mormon city, weary travelers found a welcome resting place. They could also stock up on food and supplies. Even more important, they could buy fresh horses and oxen to pull their wagons. Without healthy animals, many would have no way to continue on their journey.

John D. Lee

The huge number of non-Mormon visitors alarmed many of Salt Lake City's permanent residents. The Mormons generally looked down on the miners. They thought the forty-niners were too excited by dreams of gold. As Mormon leader John D. Lee noted, "It was the love of [money] that has caused thousands to leave their pleasant homes & comfortable Firesides & thus plunge themselves into unnecessary suffering & distress."

The Mormons were particularly wary of miners from Missouri and Illinois. Some had been part of the violent mobs that had forced the Mormons out of those states. Occasionally, the Mormon-run government of Salt Lake City found excuses to

Visiting Salt Lake

In 1849 and 1850, more than twenty-five thousand travelers passed through Salt Lake City on their way to California.

charge these travelers heavy fines. Isaac Harvey, a miner from Missouri, noted, "I knew many **emigrants** that were ruined and had to work their way to Oregon or California."

Profiting from the Trail

For the Mormons, the flood of strangers into Salt Lake City was in some ways beneficial. As the Pioneer Band had discovered, wagon trains were willing to pay hefty fares for help in traveling over rivers. The Mormons ran several successful ferrying businesses. The ferry and blacksmith shop they established along the Platte were especially good moneymakers. One visitor said the businesses were "as good a gold mine as any in California."

The Mormons also made money by trading with the forty-niners. Many miners were desperate for horses and fresh

Mormons ferry pioneers across the Platte River.

Covered wagons like this one were often overpacked, resulting in the need to get rid of belongings.

foods, such as butter and milk. They were willing to pay nearly any price to Mormon traders for these goods. At the same time, miners were eager to unload items that made their wagons too heavy. They were willing to sell off clothing, flour, gunpowder, harnesses, and even extra wagons for nearly nothing. Sometimes, the miners gave up looking for a buyer and simply dumped supplies along the trail. This trail trash was a **windfall** for poor Mormons. Gathering up what the miners had thrown away, they could get for free nearly everything they needed for a comfortable life.

The Mormons had fled west to escape contact with non-Mormons. But within a few years, their dealings with the forty-niners helped them to build a prosperous city. In the Mormons' eyes, this was all part of God's plan. He had not only led them to Great Salt Lake. He had also made the miners hungry for gold so that the Mormons could thrive.

Mormons crossing the trail to Utah with a handcart

Chapter Five

The Handcart Companies

The gold rush era brought wealth to the Mormon Church. Its leaders decided to use the church's money to help fulfill a dream of Joseph Smith's. Months after founding the church, Smith had a revelation. In it, he was told that his followers should be "gathered in unto one place upon the face of this land." Twenty years later, church leaders had enough money to gather all Mormons in one place—Salt Lake City.

To help make the gathering possible, the church established the Perpetual Emigrating Fund (PEF) in 1850. The PEF paid the travel costs of any Mormon who wanted to move to Salt Lake City. Money taken from the PEF, however, was considered a loan. Once Mormons arrived in the city with the PEF's help, they were expected to pay back everything they had borrowed.

The Gathering

In its early years, the PEF focused on the Mormons still living in Missouri. Most Missouri Mormons had traveled west years earlier, but a small number had stayed behind. Some were too poor to move, but others had become comfortable in Missouri. They were not eager to leave their homes and farms.

The church worked hard to convince the Missouri Mormons to travel west. It sent them pamphlets, saying they had a duty to join the other Mormons. The pamphlets also

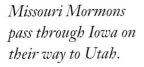

Missouri Mormons pass through Iowa on their way to Utah.

The first overseas Mormon mission was established in present-day Hawaii.

reminded them of all the sacrifices the Pioneer Band had made to blaze the Mormon Trail. One read, "We say again, come home! . . . [Y]ou can come here with greater comfort and safety than the Pioneers came here who had nothing to come to." Finally, the Missouri Mormons obeyed. In 1852, they arrived in large numbers. More Mormons traveled the Mormon Trail that year than any other.

Once the Missouri Mormons were in Salt Lake City, church leaders turned their attention to the Mormons of Europe. For decades, the church had sent **missionaries** to England, Denmark, Germany, and other European countries. They introduced Europeans to Mormonism, and many chose to convert. Most European Mormons were eager to move to the United States. A few converted just because they wanted to escape the poverty of their native lands.

For European Mormons, the trip west was long and difficult. In the early 1850s, they traveled by ship to New Orleans, Louisiana. From that port, they sailed up the Mississippi and Missouri rivers. They then began the long, hard journey over the Mormon Trail in wagon trains.

A Mormon family cooks by campfire.

Handcart Size

The typical handcart was about 3 feet (1 meter) wide, 4 feet (1.2 m) long, and 9 inches (23 cm) deep.

Traveling with Handcarts

The PEF was a great success. In fact, so many Mormons borrowed from it that soon much of the fund was spent. A crisis in Salt Lake City made the situation worse. In 1856, the Mormons' crops failed because of drought. Swarms of grasshoppers destroyed the few plants that did grow. The Mormon leaders had to spend much of the church's money to buy food for their people.

With the fund dwindling, the church looked for a less expensive way to bring Mormons west. Its leaders decided to give travelers handcarts instead of wagons. The wooden handcarts were similar to wheelbarrows. Each looked like a box on wheels, fitted with long handles that were connected across by a wooden bar. The box was just big enough to hold food and supplies needed for one person.

Traveling in large groups called companies, Mormons were to push or pull their handcarts as they walked west. Each company would also have a small herd of cows for milk and cattle for meat. The plan would not only save the church money. According to the Mormon leaders, it would also be a faster and safer way to travel the Mormon Trail.

Mormons travel by covered wagon and handcart to reach Utah.

Disaster on the Trail

In 1856, the church organized five handcart companies. The first three made the trip without any trouble. But the last two—the Willie and Martin companies—began the journey late. They set off in July, even though wagon trains usually left weeks earlier to avoid winter weather. Despite the dangers, the travelers were in high spirits. John Chislett of the Willie Company later wrote, "[W]e moved gaily forward full of hope and faith. At our camp each evening could be heard songs of joy, merry peals of laughter, and bon mots [clever remarks] on our condition and prospects."

By the time they reached Fort Laramie, however, members of the Willie Company began to worry. Winter was coming, and food was running low. Company leaders decided everyone

The Handcart Disaster

More than 220 people in the Willie and Martin companies died on the Mormon Trail.

A handcart company struggles through a storm on its trek west.

IN MEMORY OF THOSE MEMBERS OF THE WILLIE
HANDCART CO. WHOSE JOURNEY STARTED TOO LATE
AND ENDED TOO EARLY AND WERE BURIED HERE IN
A CIRCULAR GRAVE OCTOBER 24 & 25, 1856.
WILLIAM JAMES, 46   BODIL MORTINSEN, 9
ELIZABETH BAILEY, 52   NILS ANDERSON, 41
JAMES KIRKWOOD, 11   OLE MADSEN, 41
SAMUEL GADD, 10   JAMES GIBB, 67
LARS WENDIN, 60   CHESTERTON GILMAN, 66
ANNE OLSEN, 46   THOMAS GURLDSTONE, 62
ELLA NILSON, 22 JENS NILSON, 6   WILLIAM GROVES, 27

would have to move faster and eat less. But soon the snow began to fall. A sudden storm forced them to stop. Captain James G. Willie went to search for a rescue team that Brigham Young had sent to find them. Willie was gone for three days, leaving his company snowbound and starving. Chislett later wrote, "Such craving hunger I never saw before, and may God in his mercy spare me the sight again." Dozens of people froze or starved to death as they waited for Willie to return.

Finally, at dawn on the third day, the survivors saw the rescue wagons approaching. "Shouts of joy rent the air," Chislett recalled. "Strong men wept till tears ran freely down their furrowed and sunburnt cheeks, and little children . . . danced around with gladness." They reached Salt Lake City in

This marker commemorates some of the members of the Willie Company who were lost in the autumn of 1856.

Settlers pull handcarts as they migrate west.

November. The same month, the Martin Company arrived after suffering similar hardships. The ordeal of the handcart companies was one of the worst disasters in the history of the American **migration** west.

A few survivors believed their leaders had failed them and decided to leave the church. For most, though, this test of faith had only made them more **devout.** They shared the reaction of James G. Bleak of the Martin Company. After finally reaching Salt Lake City, he announced, "I . . . rejoice greatly and give praise to God for my safe arrival in Zion."

U.S. Army soldiers rest during their expedition to Utah Territory to battle the Mormons.

The Utah War

In the winter of 1857, the Mormon Trail was crowded with travelers. They were not Mormons heading to Salt Lake City or gold seekers bound for California. They were U.S. troops. President James Buchanan had sent 2,500 soldiers to battle the Mormons of Utah Territory.

Tensions had long been rising between the Mormons and the federal government. Buchanan claimed the Mormons would not obey officials appointed by the federal government. He said they were rebels plotting against the United States.

As the troops marched westward, Brigham Young prepared his own army—the Nauvoo Legion. It included more soldiers than the approaching American force. The legion tried to slow the troops by blocking the trail and setting fire to supply forts. The weather, however, became the Americans' greatest obstacle. A bitterly cold winter forced the soldiers to stop their advance. It was spring before they were able to reach Salt Lake City. By that time, Young and Buchanan had negotiated a peace treaty. The Utah War ended before the fighting could begin.

Joseph Young, the first person to successfully travel down the Mormon Trail and back in one season

Chapter Six

Down-and-Back

Despite the disaster of 1856, handcart companies continued to travel along the Mormon Trail for four more years. Mormon leaders, however, looked for a safer way to bring their followers west. In 1860, they finally found it.

In the spring of that year, Brigham Young's nephew Joseph led a train of twenty-nine wagons out of Salt Lake City. The wagon train crossed the Mormon Trail to the Missouri River. There, it picked up supplies and turned around.

A Mormon wagon train crosses the Rocky Mountains.

Within a few months, the wagon train was home.

Joseph Young had done something everyone had thought was impossible. His wagon train traveled down the Mormon Trail and back again in one season. Before Young's trip, the Mormons thought a team of oxen could not survive that journey. But Young made his trip slowly, making sure his animals got enough rest.

Heading East

Joseph Young's success inspired the Mormon leaders to develop the down-and-back system. The church began organizing wagon trains to head east down the Mormon Trail. When they reached towns along the Missouri River, they would pick up Mormon emigrants. Then the wagons would turn around and head west on the trail and bring the Mormons back to Utah Territory.

The Pony Express

The Pony Express was founded in 1860 to carry mail across the West on horseback. Part of its route was the Mormon Trail.

Church leaders asked the Mormons of Salt Lake Valley to help pay for the down-and-back wagons. They organized the Mormons into groups of several hundred people called wards. Each ward was responsible for donating enough oxen, wagons, supplies, and food for one journey down and back. The emigrants repaid the cost later.

The first down-and-back wagon trains headed out in April 1861. They were led by captains, older men skilled in traveling over rough trails. Assisting them were crews of young men, whom the Mormons nicknamed the "Mountain Boys." Many of the Mountain Boys signed up for the wagon trains to escape the hard day-to-day grind of farming. Energetic and a little wild, they far preferred the adventure of the trail.

A Mormon camp in Wyoming, with tents and wagons, in 1866

An illustration of a covered wagon train

It took about nine weeks to reach the Missouri River. The captains managed the wagon trains carefully. They made sure the animals were well-rested and the wagons were properly repaired. Each night, five or six Mountain Boys were assigned to protect the animals and supplies. After staying up all night, they spent the day trying to sleep in the wagons as they bumped down the uneven trail. Along the way, the crews dropped off goods at the supply stations. These would be used during the trip back.

The Return Trip

In early summer, the down-and-back wagons reach the eastern end of the trail. They set up camp in towns along the Missouri River. When the down-and-back system first began, they often stayed in Florence, Nebraska. The town was built at the site of Winter Quarters, the camp established in 1846 by early Mormons.

Once settled, the wagon crews met up with Mormon emigrants. Many were European. They had already survived a long journey. They had crossed the Atlantic Ocean by ship, then crossed the eastern United States by train. Boarding the down-and-back wagons, they prepared for the final leg of the difficult trip west.

Like the Pioneer Band, many travelers suffered from illness and exhaustion on the trail. But because the down-and-back system was so well-organized, their trip was generally easier. They had plenty of supplies and food. Their journey was also faster. Previous wagon trains had covered 10 to 15 miles (16 to 24 kilometers) a day. The down-and-back trains, though, could travel more than 20 miles (32 km) between dawn and dusk. Mormon travelers in the 1860s usually spent only two and a half months on the trail.

A caravan of covered wagons carrying Mormon emigrants

The down-and-back wagons followed a strict schedule. They usually arrived in Utah Territory in late fall. As the wagons rolled into Salt Lake City, the emigrants received a warm reception. Brigham Henry Roberts remembered arriving in the city when he was ten years old: "People had turned out to welcome the plains-worn emigrants and were standing on the street sides to greet them. Some horsemen dashed up the street swinging their cowboy hats."

The Trail's End

The down-and-back wagon trains proved a great success. Between 1861 and 1868, more than two thousand wagons brought about twenty thousand Mormons to Salt Lake City. But on May 10, 1869, the down-and-back system came to an abrupt end. On that day, the transcontinental railroad was completed. Railroad tracks stretched across the United States.

The completion of the transcontinental railroad marked the end of the Mormon Trail as a popular route west.

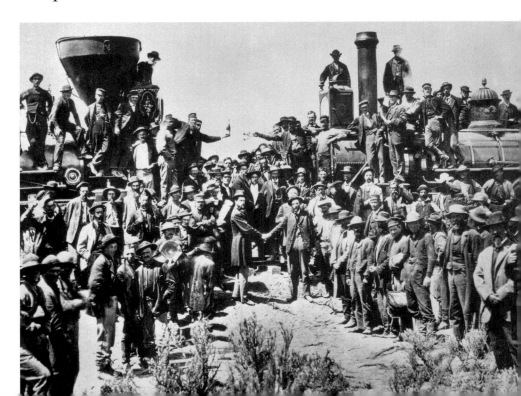

The restored jail in Carthage, Illinois, where Joseph and Hyrum Smith were killed is a site along the Mormon Pioneer National Historic Trail.

Emigrants no longer had to travel in wagon trains across the Mormon Trail to reach Utah Territory. They could travel in comfortable train cars instead. Almost overnight, traffic along the trail disappeared.

The era of the Mormon Trail was over. As time passed, private landowners took over the land where the trail had been. Still, some segments of the trail survived.

In 1978, the U.S. Congress established the Mormon Pioneer National Historic Trail. The remains of the trail are now part of the National Trails System. Tourists can travel along an auto tour route that roughly follows the historic trail through five states.

The history of the Mormon Trail is also celebrated every year by the people of the state of Utah. Every July 24, they observe Pioneer Day. It marks the anniversary of the arrival of Brigham Young and the Pioneer Band in Salt Lake Valley. During the holiday, huge parades are held in Salt Lake City, Provo, and other Utah cities. The festivities are a yearly reminder of the state's early settlers—the thousands of men and women who traveled the Mormon Trail, dreaming of a new life in the West.

Mormon Church members pull a handcart as part of a modern-day celebration of the Mormons' journey to Utah.

Timeline

1830	Joseph Smith and his followers establish the Mormon Church.
1839	The Mormons move their headquarters to Nauvoo, Illinois.
1844	Joseph Smith is murdered by an angry mob.
1845	Brigham Young announces the Mormons will leave Illinois for the West.
1846	February: Mormons flee Nauvoo and began traveling across Iowa Territory June: Mormons establish Winter Quarters.
1847	April: The Pioneer Band begins traveling west on the Mormon Trail. June: Brigham Young consults with mountain man Jim Bridger. July: The Pioneer Band enters Salt Lake Valley.
1848	Gold miners begin traveling to California; many follow the Mormon Trail.
1850	The Mormon Church establishes the Perpetual Emigration Fund to help poor Mormons move west.
1856	Five handcart companies travel west on the Mormon Trail; more than two hundred Mormons die along the way.
1861	The Mormon Church organizes the down-and-back wagon trains.
1868	September: The last down-and-back wagon train arrives in Salt Lake City.
1869	June: The first Mormons arrive in Salt Lake City by railroad, marking the end of regular traffic on the Mormon Trail.
1978	Congress establishes the Mormon Pioneer National Historic Trail.

Glossary

cholera—a disease caused by bacteria

devout—devoted to one's religion

emigrants—people who permanently move from one place to another

extermination—to get rid of by killing or destroying

ferried—carried people or things from one place to another

flimsy—thin or weak

gold rush—a sudden movement of people to an area where gold has been discovered

migration—movement from one location to another

militia—an army made up of ordinary citizens

missionaries—people who try to persuade others to adopt their religion

persecution—mistreating people because of their race, religion, or other differences

plural marriage—the Mormon practice of being married to more than one woman at the same time; non-Mormons call this illegal practice polygamy

revelation—a message believed to come from God

territory—an area in the United States governed by an appointed or elected governor that may later become a state

wagon train—a group of covered wagons carrying families traveling together on an overland trail to the American West in the mid-nineteenth century

windfall—something valuable received for free

Zion—an ideal homeland believed to be set aside by God for the faithful

To Find Out More

Books

Fiction

Cannon, A. E. *Charlotte's Rose*. New York: Wendy Lamb Books, 2002.

Izquierdo, Robyn Pearl. *Little Snowflakes: A Lesson in Love*. Denville, N.J.: X.D.I. Publishing, 1999.

Nonfiction

Madsen, Susan Arrington. *I Walked to Zion: True Stories of Young Pioneers on the Mormon Trail*. Salt Lake City: Deseret Book Company, 1994.

Nash, Carol Rust. *The Mormon Trail and the Latter-day Saints in American History.* Springfield, N.J.: Enslow Publishers, 1999.

Sanford, William R., and Carl R. Green. *Brigham Young: Pioneer and Mormon Leader.* Springfield, N.J.: Enslow Publishers, 1996.

Organizations and Online Sites

The Church of Jesus Christ of Latter-day Saints
http://www.lds.org
The official site of the Mormon Church offers a wealth of information about Mormon history and beliefs.

Mormon Pioneer National Historic Trail
http://www.nps.gov/mopi/
This site, operated by the National Park Service, gives a brief description of the historic trail and lists organizations to contact for more information.

Historic Nauvoo
Main and Young Street
Nauvoo, IL 62354
http://www.historicnauvoo.net/hnauvoo/
Visit the historic town of Nauvoo, Illinois, to learn more about Mormon history.

Mormon Trail Center at Historic Winter Quarters
3215 State Street
Omaha, NE 68112
Learn more about the Mormon Trail at this visitor's center located at historic Winter Quarters.

Museum of Church History and Art
The Church of Jesus Christ of Latter-day Saints
45 North West Temple Street
Salt Lake City, UT 84150
http://www.lds.org/churchhistory/museum
Mormon art and artifacts can be viewed at this museum.

A Note on Sources

The story of the Mormon Trail has inspired a vast amount of literature. The most eloquent account of the trail's development and the Mormons' plight is *The Gathering of Zion: The Story of the Mormon Trail* (Reprint, University of Nebraska Press, 1992) by famed western writer Wallace Stegner. For a solid introduction to the trail's history from the Mormon perspective, I've found the documentary *Trail of Hope: The Story of the Mormon Trail* (Videotape, BWE Utah, 1997) extremely useful. The accompanying book of the same title (Shadow Mountain, 1997) features an insightful text by William W. Slaughter and Michael Landon. In addition to offering a wealth of excerpts from diaries and other primary sources, this book is filled with well-chosen photographs that vividly recall life on the trail. Anyone interested in visiting sites on the trail would be well served by William E. Hill's *The Mormon Trail: Yesterday and Today* (Utah State University

Press, 1996). Along with a concise history of the trail in words, maps, and photographs, Hill provides an exhaustive list of historic sites associated with the trail. For the dramatic story of the Mormon handcart companies, the most comprehensive source is *Handcarts to Zion: The Story of a Unique Western Migration, 1856–1860* (Reprint, University of Nebraska Press, 1992) by Ann W. Hafen and LeRoy C. Hafen. I'd also recommend John Unruh's *The Plains Across: The Overland Emigrants and the Trans-Mississippi West, 1840-60* (Reprint, University of Illinois Press, 1993). This classic work of western history helps put the experience of travelers along the Mormon Trail in the context of the broader western migration during the mid-nineteenth century.

—*Liz Sonneborn*

Index

Numbers in *italics* indicate illustrations.

About the Author

Liz Sonneborn is a writer and an editor, living in Brooklyn, New York. A graduate of Swarthmore College, she has written more than fifty books for children and adults, including *The American West*, *A to Z of American Women in the Performing Arts*, and *The New York Public Library's Amazing Native American History*, winner of a 2000 Parent's Choice Award.